Copy this Poem

Fuzzy Wuzzy was a bear.

Fuzzy Wuzzy had no hair.

Fuzzy wasn't very fuzzy.

Was he?

Find the Words

✕ and   _____ ten
_____ green   _____ the
_____ in   _____ three
_____ of   _____ to
_____ red

the	to	and	three
the	of	and	the
the	to	at	three
ten	to	and	three
to	the	and	to
of	of	as	three
the	to	and	three

Parents: Point to each word and say it for your child. Have him/her repeat the word back to you.

is   you

that   it

blue   yellow

six   nine

Fill in the boxes:

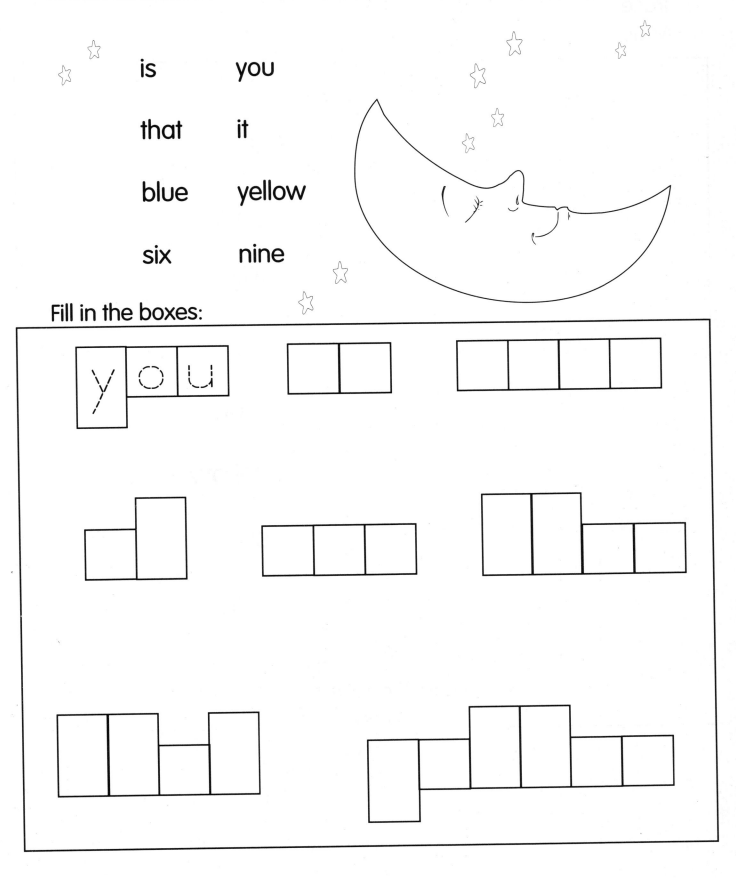

Trace.
Match.

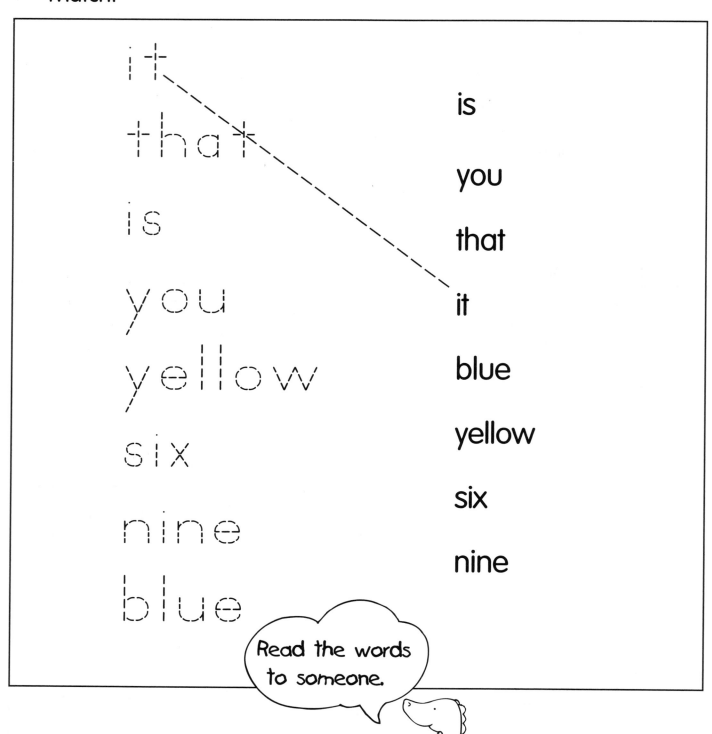

it

that

is

you

yellow

six

nine

blue

is

you

that

it

blue

yellow

six

nine

Read the words to someone.

Identifying key vocabulary words

Unscramble the words.

is	you
that	it
blue	yellow
six	nine

| t i | _i t_ |
| x i s | _ _ _ _ |

| s i | _ _ _ _ |
| y u o | _ _ _ _ |

Match.

is ———————— The
the   It
that   Is
it   That

Draw.

six yellow

nine blue

Read and color.

The 🩳 is blue.

Is that you?

That 🐰 is in a ☐ .

It is yellow.

Read the words to someone.

Parents: Explain to your child that words at the beginning of a sentence start with a capital letter.

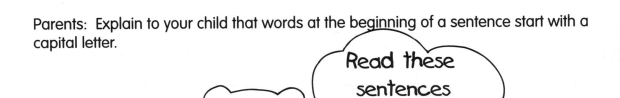

Read these sentences to someone.

a - A   the - The   it - It

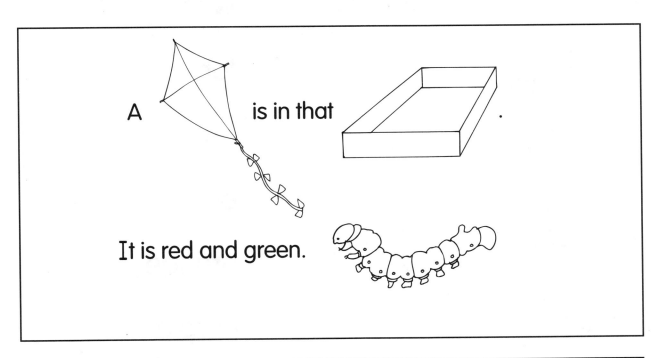

A [kite] is in that [box] .

It is red and green. [caterpillar]

The [girl] is six.

The [cake] is yellow and blue.

Trace.
Match.

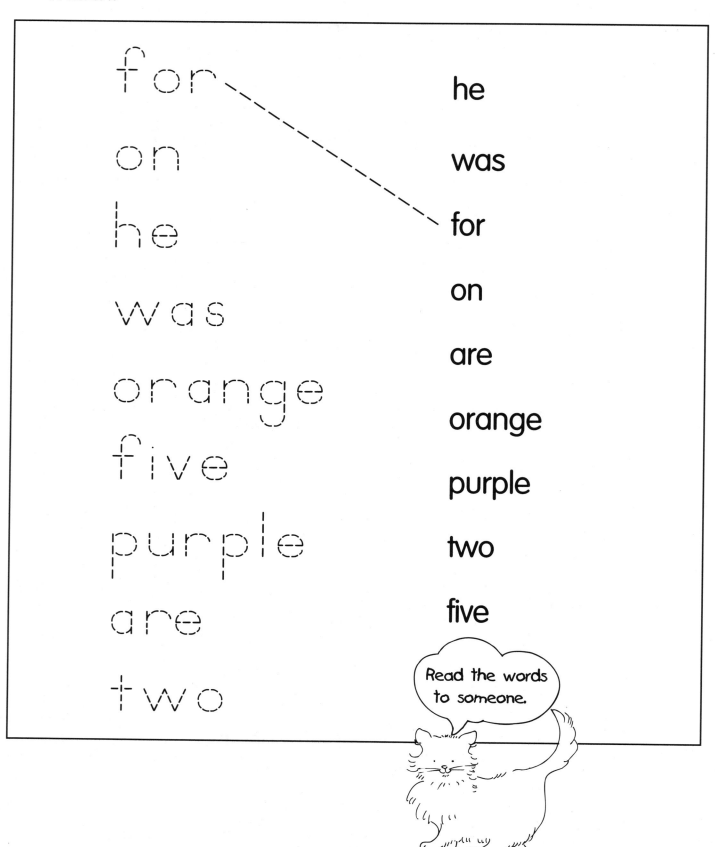

for   he

on   was

he   for

was   on

orange   are

five   orange

purple   purple

are   two

two   five

Read the words to someone.

Identifying key vocabulary words

How to Make an Ice Cream Cone

1. Read 2. Cut 3. Paste in order	
	1
	2
	3
	4

Take a big lick
and gobble it down.

Then get the ice cream
from the freezer.

First get a scoop
and a cone.

Take a big scoop
of ice cream and
put it on the cone.

Fill this ice cream cone.

How many scoops do you have?

What flavors do you have?

_____

- - - - - - - - - - - - - - - - -

_____

_____

- - - - - - - - - - - - - - - - -

_____

_____

- - - - - - - - - - - - - - - - -

_____

_____

- - - - - - - - - - - - - - - - -

_____

as   with   his

they   I   black

white   one   eight

Fill in the boxes:

b l a c k

Trace.
Match.

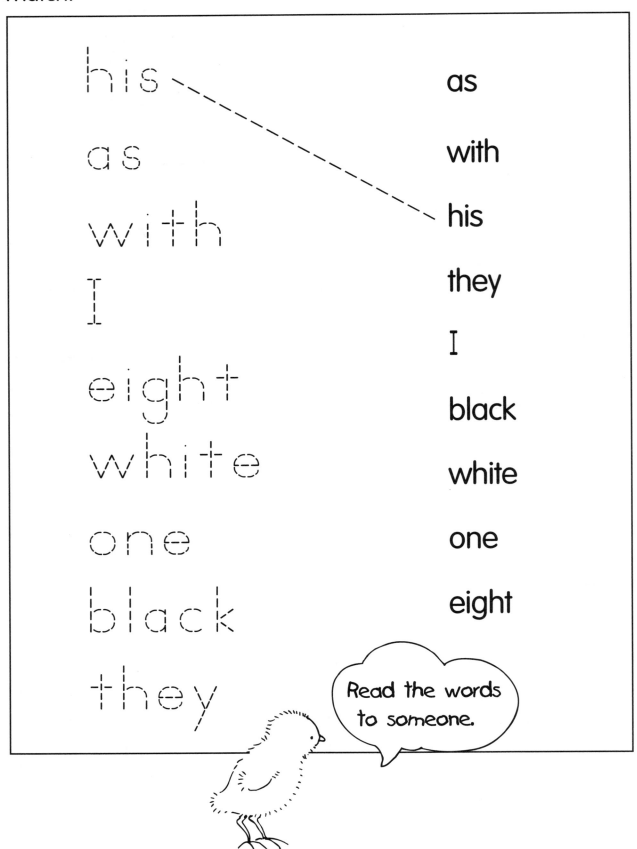

his

as

with

I

eight

white

one

black

they

as

with

his

they

I

black

white

one

eight

Read the words to someone.

Read and color.

white with black ●

His blue 🌂.

I am the 🤡.

a black 🐜

Read the words to someone.

Find the Words

X̶ as   ____ with   ____ his
____ they   ____ black   ____ white
____ one   ____ eight

```
b  l  a  c  k  h  i  s (a)
e  i  g  h  t  o  n  e (s)
t  h  e  y  w  h  i  t  e
w  i  t  h  g  r  e  e  n
```

they	with	eight	one
(they)	white	they	and
they	with	eight	one
that	with	eight	one
two	was	white	of
they	with	eight	one
they	white	they	one

How to Wrap a Gift

1
2
3
4
5
6

Wrap the box in pretty paper.	Set the gift in a box.
Now put on the lid.	Tape a ribbon on the box.
Stick a card under the ribbon.	Take the gift to the party.

Draw what is in the box?

Who would you give the gift to? ———————————————————————————

Parents: Point to each word and say it for your child. Have him/her repeat the word back to you.

at	be	this
have	from	brown
four	seven	she

Fill in the boxes:

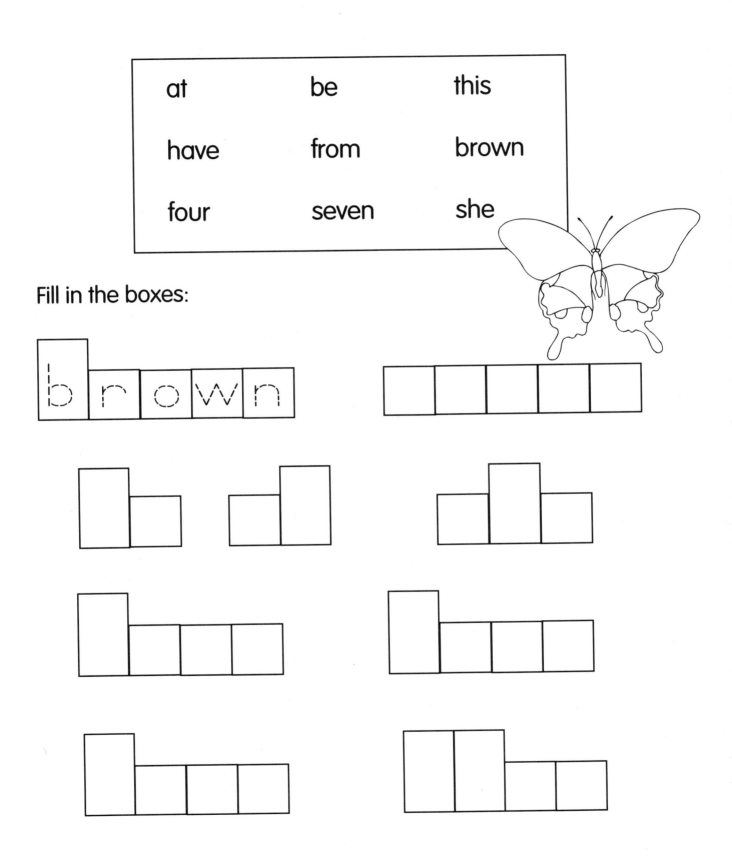

Read the words to someone.

the	of	red	one
a	to	green	two
and	in	blue	three
in	is	yellow	four
you	they	orange	five
that	I	purple	six
it	at	black	seven
was	be	white	eight
for	this	brown	nine
on	have		ten
he	from		
are	she		
as	with		
his			

I can read _____ words.

Match:

6

m

s

g

h

m s g h

<u>m</u>ouse

__ock

__oat

__en

Mark the words that rhyme.

hog   ~~at~~   oat

Write the rhyming words.

dock	hill	Muffet	clock	sheep
day	Peep	away	tuffet	Jill

1. Jack and _____

   Went up the _____.

2. Little Bo _____

   Has lost her _____.

3. Hickory, dickory, _____

   The mouse ran up the _____.

4. Little Miss _____

   Sat on a _____.

5. Rain, rain go _____

   Come again another _____.

Color the words that rhyme with:

funny 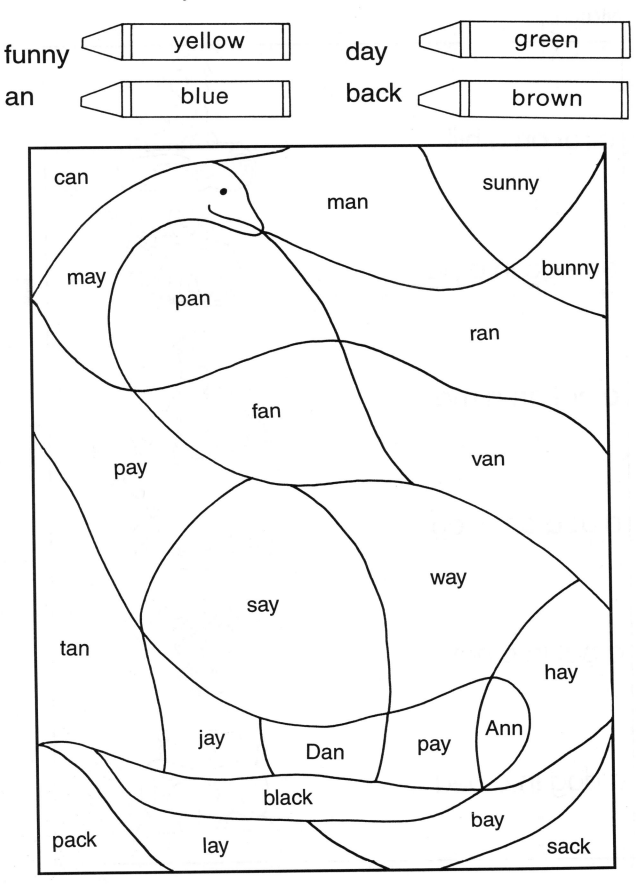 yellow   day green

an blue   back brown

can

man

sunny

may

bunny

pan

ran

fan

van

pay

way

say

tan

hay

jay

Ann

Dan

pay

black

bay

pack

lay

sack

Read.
Match.

a rat on a hill

an egg in a pan

a hat on a man

a dog on a log

a bat in a net

a dog in a bed

Read.
Match.

The cat is fat.

The dog can run.

The fox is red.

The bed is big.

The man is hot.

The ant sat.

This

the

The Pond

This is a big pond.

A log is in the pond.

A frog is on the log.

Jump, frog, jump.

I read this story to_____.

Draw:

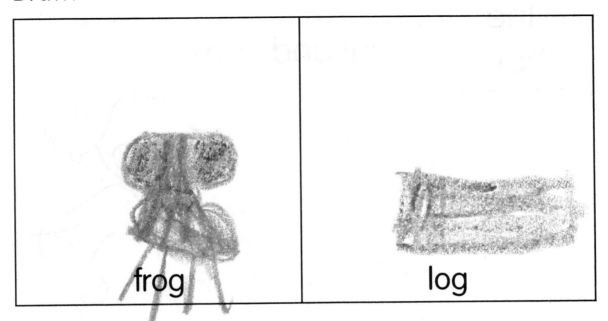

| frog | log |

Fill in:

The pond is __big__ .

A __log__ is in the pond.

A __FROG__ is on the log.

Pat and Sam

Sam digs in the mud.

Sam is a mess.

Pat is mad!

"Sam must get a bath."

I read this story to_____.

Match:

Pat

mud

bath

Sam

Sam digs in _____ .

Pat is _____ .

Sam must get a _____ .

Note: Explain to your learner what usually happens when you add a **silent e** to a short vowel word. The vowel becomes a long sound.

Silent e

Read.	Add an e and read.	
can	can e̲	
cub	cub ___	
bit	bit ___	
tap	tap ___	
kit	kit ___	
rob	rob ___	

Color the Puzzle

blue	yellow	red
<u>ai</u>	<u>oa</u>	<u>ee</u>

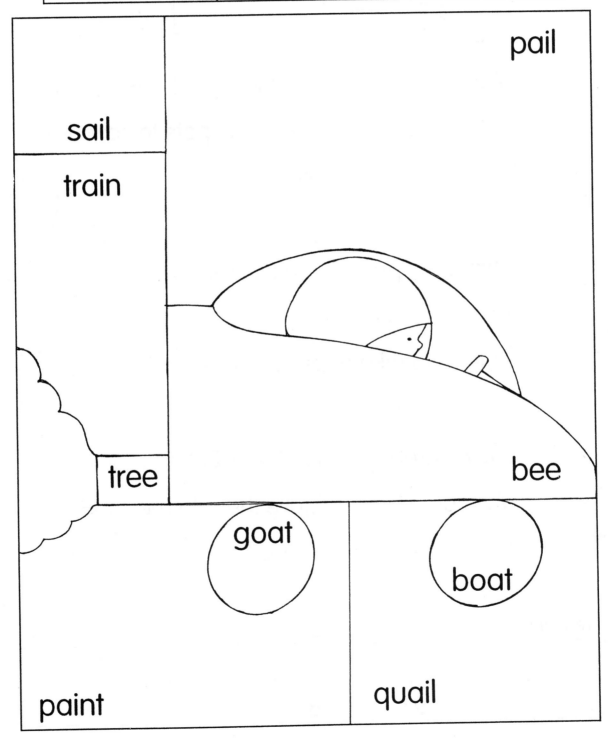

sail

train

pail

tree

bee

goat

boat

paint

quail

Pets at School

"Wake up, Eve," said June.

"Miss Lane said we can take pets to school.

I don't want to be late."

"This is my pet cat," said June.

"His name is Dave.

He likes to take naps on my bed."

"I have three pet mice," said Zeke.

"My mom and dad gave them to me.

My mice like to eat seeds."

I read this story to _____.

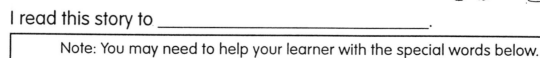

Note: You may need to help your learner with the special words below.
said   school   this
want   have

"This is my dog, Mike," said Kate.
"Sit, Mike. Shake my hand.
He wants a bone to eat."

"I have a pet," said Miss Lane.
It is long and has scales.
"It is a black snake!"

We had fun with the pets at school.

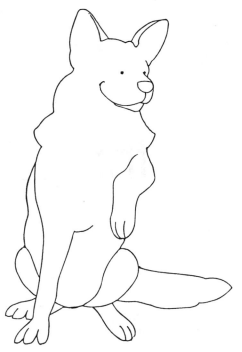

I read this story to _____.

Read the story again.
Circle the long vowel words.

"Wake up, Eve."

Note: Two vowels together can make a long vowel sound.

bee

 tr e e

 j _ _ p

 thr _ _

 _ _ l

 kn _ _

Read these words to someone.

How to Take a Bath

1. Read 2. Cut 3. Paste in order	
	1
	2
	3
	4
	5
	6

Add bubble bath.	Get dressed.
Get out of the tub and dry off.	Get into the tub.
Fill the tub with water.	Wash with soap and a rag.

Why do you have to take baths?

_____

_ _

_____

_____

_ _

_____

_____

_ _

_____

Do you like a bath or a shower best? _____

Do you like bubble bath in your tub? _____

Skill: can write the letters of the alphabet correctly and neatly

a b c d e f g h i j k l m
n o p q r s t u v w x y z

Skill: identifies the consonant digraphs **ch**, **sh**, **wh**, and **th** and can give the sound each one represents

chip   **sh**op   **wh**at   **th**is

Color the pictures.

ch – blue   **sh** – red
wh – green   **th** – brown

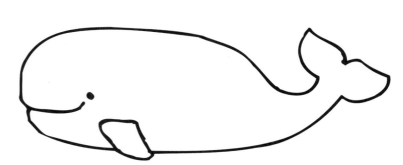

Read these words to someone.

the   with
then   bath

Skill: identifies and uses correct capitalization of the first word of a sentence

The sun is hot.

Fill in the capital letters.

M
1. ~~m~~y pet is not big.

2. it can run and hop.

3. my pet can swim.

4. he is a green pet.

5. his name is Hopper.

6. can you tell what my pet is?

Skill: recognizes correct word order in a sentence

run. can I

I can run.

Put the words in order.
Read the sentence.

1. cat   had   The   nap.   a

The cat had a nap.

2. rat   run   Did   the   and   hide?

_____

3. see   six   I   ducks.   yellow

_____

4. Bob   and   had   Tom   fun.

_____

Skill: identifies and uses correct punctuation at the end of asking and telling sentences
- A **period** goes at the end of a sentence that **tells**.
- A **question mark** goes at the end of a sentence that **asks** a question.

The fox is here. Do you see a fox**?**

Put in the **.** and **?**

1. The dog had a nap**.**

2. Is that a fox

3. Can you run fast

4. A cat is on my bed

5. Will the duck get wet

6. What is that

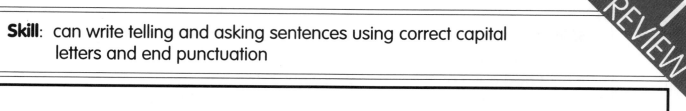

Write a sentence that **tells** about this monkey.

_____

_ _

_____

Write a sentence that **asks** a question about the monkey.

_____

_ _

_____

Skill: alphabetizes words through the first letter

ant	**b**ell
box	**g**o
cat	**n**ot

a b c d e f g h i j k l m n o p q r s t u v w x y z

Put the words in **a b c** order.

1. _____

2. _____

3. _____

cat

ant

box

1. _____

2. _____

3. _____

kite

jam

nest

1. _____

2. _____

3. _____

zebra

skunk

whale

Skill: draw conclusions from given facts

The sky is dark.
Water is falling from the sky.
Conclusion: It is raining.

Circle the answer.

1. I get a can.
I take the lid off.
I put food in a dish.
I am feeding the...?

2. I get a rag.
I get soap.
I get a tub.
I am washing...?

3. It is cold.
Snow comes down.
The wind blows.
I put on...?

4. I am sad.
I made a mess.
It is hard to clean.
I spilled...?

Skill: identifies and uses naming words (**nouns**)

A **noun** names a person, place, or thing.

Tom   school   hat

Put a ring around the **naming** words.

1. (Dad) has a (box) in the (car.)

2. Ted got a red kite and a blue ball.

3. The bike is at the park.

4. Six dogs ran up the street.

5. That cup has milk in it.

6. Mom and Dad went to school.

Name the things in this picture.

Skill: identifies plural nouns ending in **s**

one - cat

more than one - cat**s**

Write.

Skill: identifies and uses action words (**verbs**)

A **verb** tells what the subject is doing.

run   sing   jump

Put a line under **doing** words.

1. Tom <u>rides</u> his bike.

2. The cat sleeps on a rug.

3. A green frog hops to the pond.

4. Matt played with his dog.

5. I skip and jump.

6. Kim painted a fish.

Draw what you can do.

Skill: identifies and uses words that describe

big   hot   six   red

Put a ring around the word that describes.
Match the words and pictures.

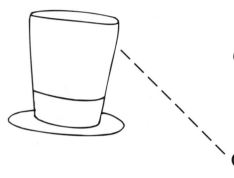

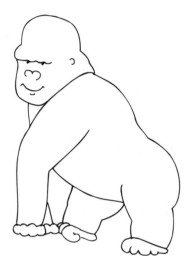

a big ape

a tall hat

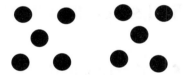

a red hen

a wet mop

ten dots

a soft cat

Answer Key

Please take time to go over the work your child has completed. Ask your child to explain what he/she has done. Praise both success and effort. If mistakes have been made, explain what the answer should have been and how to find it. Let your child know that mistakes are a part of learning. The time you spend with your child helps let him/her know you feel learning is important.

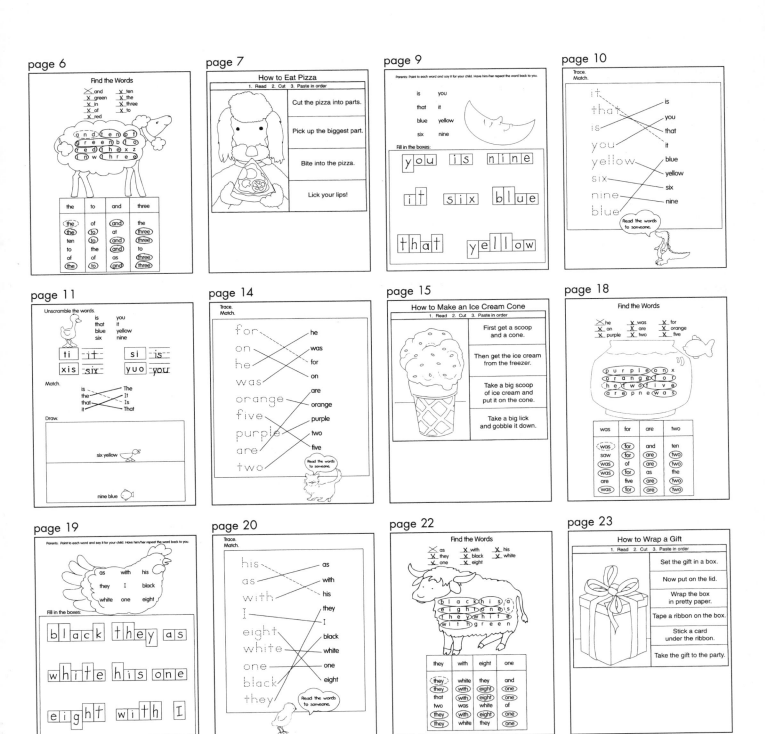

page 25

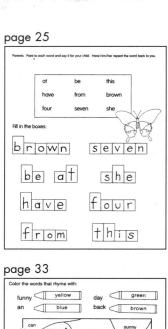

Parents: Point to each word and say it for your child. Have him/her repeat the word back to you.

at	be	this
have	from	brown
four	seven	she

Fill in the boxes:

b r o w n   s e v e n

b e   a t   s h e

h a v e   f o u r

f r o m   t h i s

page 27

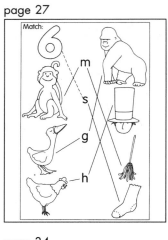

Match:

6 m s g h

page 28

m s g h

mouse

sock

goat

hen

page 32

Write the rhyming words.

dock   hill   Muffet   clock   sheep
day   Peep   away   tuffet   Jill

1. Jack and Jill
   Went up the hill

2. Little Bo Peep
   Has lost her sheep

3. Hickory, dickory, dock
   The mouse ran up the clock

4. Little Miss Muffet
   Sat on a tuffet

5. Rain, rain go away
   Come again another day

page 33

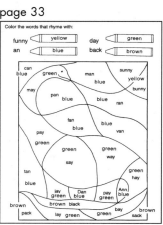

Color the words that rhyme with:

funny — yellow   day — green
an — blue   back — brown

page 34

Read.
Match.

a rat on a hill
an egg in a pan
a hat on a man
a dog on a log
a bat in a net
a dog in a bed

page 35

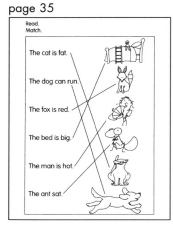

Read.
Match.

The cat is fat.
The dog can run.
The fox is red.
The bed is big.
The man is hot.
The ant sat.

page 37

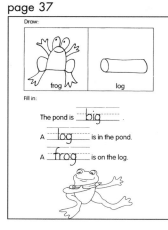

Draw:

frog   log

Fill in:

The pond is big
A log is in the pond.
A frog is on the log.

page 39

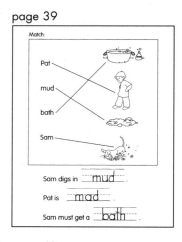

Match:

Pat
mud
bath
Sam

Sam digs in mud
Pat is mad
Sam must get a bath

page 40

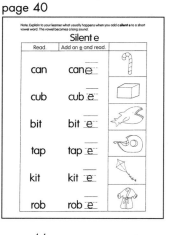

Note: Explain to your learner what usually happens when you add a silent e to a short vowel word. The vowel becomes a long vowel.

Silent e

Read.	Add an e and read.	
can	cane	
cub	cube	
bit	bite	
tap	tape	
kit	kite	
rob	robe	

page 41

Yes or No

He is in the cage.   yes
Five eggs are on the plate.   no
Feed me a bone.   no
Kate can ride the bike.   yes

page 42

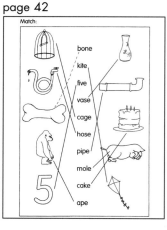

Match:

bone
kite
five
vase
cage
hose
pipe
mole
cake
ape

page 43

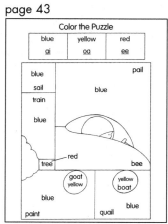

Color the Puzzle

| blue | yellow | red |
| ai | oa | ee |

blue — pail
sail
train
blue
red
tree — bee
goat yellow
yellow boat
blue
paint   quail   blue

page 44

Pets at School

"Wake up, Eve," said June.
"Miss Lane said we can take pets to school."
"I don't want to be late."

"This is my pet cat," said June.
"His name is Dave."
"He likes to take naps on my bed."

"I have three pet mice," said Zeke.
"My mom and dad gave them to me."
"My mice like to eat seeds."

I read this story to _____

Note: You may need to help your learner with the special words below.
said   school   this
want   have

page 45

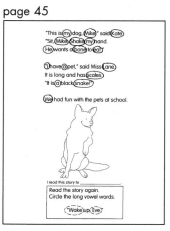

"This is my dog, Mike," said Kate.
"Sit, Mike. Shake my hand.
He wants a bone to eat."

"I have a pet," said Miss Lane.
"It is long and has scales."
"It is a black snake!"

We had fun with the pets at school.

I read this story to _____
Read the story again.
Circle the long vowel words.

"Wake up, Eve."

page 46

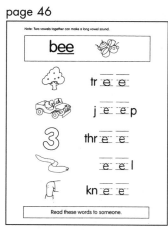

Note: Two vowels together can make a long vowel sound.

bee

tree
jeep
three
eel
knee

Read these words to someone.

page 47

How to Take a Bath

1. Read 2. Cut 3. Paste in order

	Fill the tub with water.
	Add bubble bath.
	Get into the tub.
	Wash with soap and a rag.
	Get out of the tub and dry off.
	Get dressed.

page 49

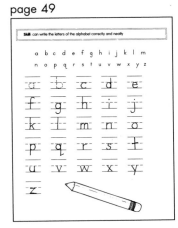

Skill: can write the letters of the alphabet correctly and neatly

a b c d e f g h i j k l m
n o p q r s t u v w x y z

a b c d e
f g h i j
k l m n o
p q r s t
u v w x y
z

page 50

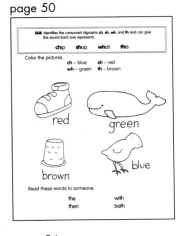

Skill: identifies the consonant digraphs ch, sh, wh, and th and can give the sound each one represents

chip   shop   what   this

Color the pictures.

ch – blue   sh – red
wh – green   th – brown

red

green

brown   blue

Read these words to someone.

the   with
then   bath

page 51

Skill: identifies and uses correct capitalization of the first word of a sentence

The sun is hot.

Fill in the capital letters.

M
1. my pet is not big.

I
2. i can run and hop.

M
3. my pet can swim.

H
4. he is a green pet.

H
5. his name is Hopper.

C
6. can you tell what my pet is?

page 52

Skill: recognizes correct word order in a sentence

run, can I

I can run.

Put the words in order.
Read the sentence.

1. cat had The nap. a
   The cat had a nap.

2. rat run Did the and hide?
   Did the rat run and hide?

3. see six I ducks. yellow
   I see six yellow ducks.

4. Bob and had Tom fun.
   Bob and Tom had fun.

page 53

Skill: identifies and uses correct punctuation at the end of asking and telling sentences
• A **period** goes at the end of a sentence that **tells**.
• A **question mark** goes at the end of a sentence that **asks** a question.

The fox is here. Do you see a fox?

Put in the . and ?

1. The dog had a nap.
2. Is that a fox?
3. Can you run fast?
4. A cat is on my bed.
5. Will the duck get wet?
6. What is that?

page 54

Skill: can write telling and asking sentences using correct capital letters and end punctuation

Write a sentence that **tells** about this monkey.

answers will vary

Write a sentence that **asks** a question about the monkey.

page 55

Skill: alphabetizes words through the first letter

ant	bell
box	go
cat	not

a b c d e f g h i j k l m n o p q r s t u v w x y z

Put the words in a b c order.

1. ant — cat
2. box — ant
3. cat — box

1. jam — kite
2. kite — jam
3. nest — nest

1. skunk — zebra
2. whale — skunk
3. zebra — whale

page 56

Parents: You may read this to your child and have him/her give you the answer or have your child read it on his/her own.

Skill: draw conclusions from given facts

The sky is dark.
Water is falling from the sky.
Conclusion: It is raining.

Circle the answer.

1. I get a can.
   I take the lid off.
   I put food in a dish.
   I am feeding the...?

2. I get a rag.
   I get soap.
   I get a tub.
   I am washing...?

3. It is cold.
   Snow comes down.
   The wind blows.
   I put on...?

4. I am sad.
   I made a mess.
   It is hard to clean.
   I spilled...?

page 57

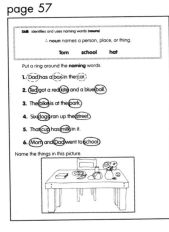

Skill: identifies and uses naming words (nouns)

A **noun** names a person, place, or thing.

Tom   school   hat

Put a ring around the naming words.

1. Dad has a box in the car.
2. Ted got a red kite and a blue ball.
3. The bike is at the park.
4. Six dogs ran up the street.
5. That cup has milk in it.
6. Mom and Dad went to school.

Name the things in this picture.

page 58

Skill: identifies plural nouns ending in s

one - cat
more than one - cats

Write.

dogs

cup

cups

bats

bat

dog

page 59

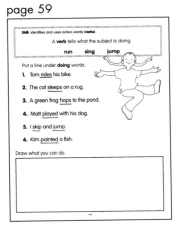

Skill: identifies and uses action words (verbs)

A **verb** tells what the subject is doing.

run   sing   jump

Put a line under doing words.

1. Tom rides his bike.
2. The cat sleeps on a rug.
3. A green frog hops to the pond.
4. Matt played with his dog.
5. I skip and jump.
6. Kim painted a fish.

Draw what you can do.

page 60

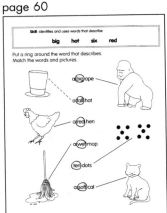

Skill: identifies and uses words that describe

big   hot   six   red

Put a ring around the word that describes.
Match the words and pictures.

a big ape
a tall hat
a red hen
a wet mop
ten dots
a soft cat

63   Answers